DATE DUE	
JAN 2 5 1997	FEB 2 0 2003
FEB 2 0 1997	FEB 2 8 2004
AUG 1 9 1997	
MAY 2 3 1998	
DEC 2 8 1998	
JAN 0 6 1999	
APR 0 2 2000	
OCT 2 2 2000	
OCT 0 8 2001	
JAN 0 7 2002	
JUN 2 2 2002	
FEB 0 8 2003	

GAYLORD   PRINTED IN U.S.A.

By Mustafa El-Amin

Published by

El-Amin Productions
P.O. Box 32148
Newark, N.J. 07102

3rd Printing

Table Of Contents

DEDICATION
ACKNOWLEDGEMENTS
INTRODUCTION

DEDICATION

This work is dedicated to the cause of Al-Islam and to those courageous men and women who are trying very hard to give an accurate representation of the religion of Al-Islam.

It is also dedicated to those early Pioneers, who braved the hardships of injustice and brutality; never giving up the struggle to make a better way of life for our people.

Last but not least, this work is dedicated to Muhammad Ali, three-time heavy weight champion, a devout Muslim and honorable man who continues to make enormous contributions to his people and society.

ACKNOWLEDGEMENTS

I would like to express my thanks and appreciation to all those who assisted me in completing this work; My wife, Wafiyyah El-Amin for typing the original manuscript; and for her patience and encouragement. Brother Umar Bey Ali and Ansari Nadir for their loyalty and advice.

INTRODUCTION

It is essential that the American people in general and the African Americans in particular know and realize that there are very clear differences in the teachings of the Universal Religion of Islam and the teachings of the Nation of Islam. In order for people to make an accurate and clear judgement or decision about anyone or anything, it is always best for them to have as much correct information as possible.

For about fifty years the teachings of the Nation of Islam was the dominant message in America(Concerning Islam and the Muslims). Most people, particularly African Americans, saw the teachings of the Nation of Islam as "The Pure Message of Islam."

However upon the death of Elijah Muhammad and the assuming of leadership by his son Wallace D. Mohammed, the old message of the Nation of Islam began to fade away and a new message and teaching came into existence. The Honorable Elijah Muhammad said this would happen. In the book Our Savior has Arrived, he writes:

> As I have pointed out to you in the
> prophecy that He will make all things new, I
> have pointed out to you that this includes our
> being given a new mind which produces new
> ideas. The new mind and the new ideas are
> to condition us for the new materialistic things
> that he will make. (p. 130-1)

He also explained how the new leader could or would make changes. "The first way to bring about something new is to change the way of thinking of the people. When you have removed from the people the old mind and idea then you can insert new ideas into their minds. This is done by the old being attracted by a new way of teaching...a new school of learning to condition their minds to that thing that you are about to present to them that is altogether new and different from what they have been accustomed to...He could use nothing of the old world..."(p.121-2) "ALLAH-U-AKBAR" One of the first things that Wallace D. Mohammed said when he became leader was "Put away your books and lessons."

The new message was/is based on the Holy Quran and Sunnah (Way) of Prophet Muhammad Ibn Abdullah, the last Messenger of Allah. It is not a completely new message or teaching in the sense that it has never been taught or heard in the world before; but it was called "New" because it was new to the ears of the members of the Nation of Islam. They never heard the pure and true teachings of Islam before (here in America).

The majority of the members of the former NOI was able to grasp the new message and have changed and accepts the Religion of Islam as it is practiced by one billion Muslims. However, the majority of the American people have still not had the same opportunity to hear the clear message of Al-Islam. Most African Americans are still deprived and denied the opportunity to hear the true teachings of Islam.

In the last five years or so there seems to be an attempt by the media and others to re-establish the former Nation of Islam and its teachings. The media has played a major role in publicizing Minister Farrakhan and his teachings. Minister Farrakhan has continuously spread the teachings of the NOI, with the help of the white media. As a result, the majority of the public are only receiving the teachings of the Nation of Islam. The people need to know the difference. That is our purpose in writing this book.

It is our aim and intent to make clear some of the fine differences that exists in the teachings of the NOI and the Religion of Al- Islam. I pray that Allah(God) will bless us to achieve our goal and keep our intentions sincere and honorable.

The information provided herein is based on the Holy Quran, and other Islamic materials as well as four books published by the NOI. They are 1. <u>Message to the Blackman</u> 2. <u>Supreme Wisdom: Solution to the So-Called Negroe's Problem</u> 3. <u>How to Eat to Live: Book 2</u> 4. <u>Our Savior has Arrived.</u> Each of these books were written by the honorable Elijah Muhammad, the former leader of the Nation of Islam.

CHAPTER ONE
HISTORY

Brief History of Al-Islam

The Religion of Al-Islam, as it is practiced today by one billion people is as ancient as the earth. The Holy Quran, the Holy book of the Muslims, says that Al-Islam is the religion of nature itself. It is the origin of life. It is called Deen-al-Fitr. Muslims believe it was the religion of the first man, Adam, as well as the way of life of all the prophets. Al-Islam means peace and submission to Allah (God). However, according to the Holy Quran and many of the Islamic Scholars, the religion of Al-Islam was fully established and perfected as a systematic way of life about 1400 years ago by Prophet Muhammad (Peace Be Upon Him) the son of Abdullah.

According to authentic history, Prophet Muhammad (PBUH) worked hard and struggled for twenty-three years to establish the religion of Al- Islam. Prophet Muhammad (PBUH) is not the founder of the Religion of Al-Islam. Al-Islam existed long before Prophet Muhammad (PBUH). Allah (God) is the author of Al-Islam. All Muslims know this. No Muslim will say Prophet Muhammad (PBUH) is the founder of Al-Islam. The Holy Quran and the Religion of Al-Islam was revealed to Prophet Muhammad (PBUH) in Arabia about 1400 years ago. He was chosen as the last Messenger and Prophet of Allah. He was given the task of bringing Al-Islam to the Arabs and the world.

Prophet Muhammad (PBUH) is a descendant of Is-mael, the son of Abraham and the Black, Egyptian woman, Hagar.

Brief History of The Nation of Islam

The Nation of Islam is a recent invention. It was started in America, Detroit, Michigan in 1930. According

1

to the teachings' of the Nation of Islam its founder is not Allah (God), the Creator of the heavens and the earth. The author and founder of the Nation of Islam was a man named Wali Fard Muhammad. Also called W.D. Fard. His message is not rooted in the essence of man and nature. It was/is not for all people. It is reproted that he came from the East to America by himself on July 4th, 1930. He preached and taught a strange doctrine in and around Detroit for about three and a half years. Before he left he taught a man named Elijah Poole(who later changed his name to Elijah Muhammad). He appointed Elijah as his spokesman and representative. He instructed Elijah to read 104 books on Prophet Muhammad Ibn Abdullah (PBUH) and Al-Islam. Elijah was left with the responsibility of building and establishing the Nation of Islam in America.

The Nation of Islam grew and attracted hundreds of thousands of African American people. Two of its most outstanding attractions were Malcolm X and Muhammad Ali. The positive accomplishments of the Nation of Islam is well documented by Sociologists, Educators,and Historians, both Black and White.

CHAPTER TWO
THE CONCEPT OF GOD

The Religion of Islam's Concept of God

> It is Allah who is
> God in heaven and God
> on earth and He is full of
> wisdom and knowledge(43:84)

Allah(God) according to the Religion of Islam, is the Creator of the heavens and the earth. He is in total charge of the entire creation. He has no beginning or ending. He was never born and will never die. He has always been in existence. Allah is not a physical being. The Holy Quran states,"No vision can grasp Him, but His grasp is over all vision and He is above total comprehension, yet He is well acquainted with all things." The Holy Quran also states, "Say He is Allah, the one and only; God the eternal, absolute; He begeteth not, nor is He begotten; and there is none like unto Him."(Chapter 112)

The Religion of Al-Islam teaches that Allah(God) is one and He has no sons or daughters. He never married anyone or had sex with anyone. He just says "Be and it is." Allah(God) is responsible for the creation of every human being. He created all colors and made our features beautiful. The concept of God in Al-Islam is an extremely vast and important concept. Perhaps the most important aspect is the belief in the Oneness(Tauheed) of God. Al-Islam teaches that Allah (God) is not a man or a woman. He is the source of human life and gender. This is very different from the belief and teachings of the Nation of Islam.

The Nation of Islam's Concept of Allah(God)

"God is a man and we just cannot make Him other than a man, lest we make Him an inferior one; for man's intelligence has no equal in other than man."(p. 6,Message to the Blackman).

3

The God of the Nation of Islam is called Master Fard Muhammad, a man who was born in 1877. "We believe that Allah(God) came in the person of Master FardMuhammad July 4, 1930." (See Final Call Newspaper)   On page 4 of the book How to Eat to Live it reads, Master Fard Muhammad, to Whom Praise are due forever, comes to prolong our lives..." In the book, Our Savior Has Arrived it reads, "He Master Fard Muhammad, God in Person." (p. 110) We also find in the book The Supreme Wisdom: Solution to the So-called Negroes' Problem (p. 11) "Allah came to us from the Holy city of Mecca, Arabia in 1930. He used the name of Wallace D. Fard, often signing it W.D. Fard. In the third year(1933) He signed his name W.F. Muhammad, which stands for Wallace Fard Muhammmad. He came alone."

The Nation of Islam's teachings concerning Allah(God) is very different from that of the Religion of Al-Islam. This fact is acknowledged on page 67 of the book Our Savior Has Arrived. There we find the following statement,"The Muslims worship one God-Allah. 'Say: He Allah is one God.' Yet 99% of the old world Muslims think that Allah is only a spirit and is not a man."

According to the teachings of the Nation of Islam, there are/were several Gods from the beginning of time. The Nation of Islam teaches that God lives and dies and passes their knowledge and god-ship from one to another. The Nation of Islam teaches that God is a man and He always was a man. (Message to the Blackman) He created Himself from and out of total triple darkness(The First God).

The Nation of Islam teaches that the Blackman is God. It teaches that one God created the moon and another one created the sun, stars, and earth. According to the teachings of the Nation of Islam, about seventy trillion years ago, one of the Black Gods got angry and tried to destroy the earth with "High explosives." However, he was unsuccessful in

4

destroying the entire earth, but he did blow it in half. The part that was separated is the moon. (If the reader has any doubt about this, read <u>Message to the Blackman</u> or ask any minister of the NOI.

The God of the Nation of Islam marries, has sex, makes mistakes, eats food and makes babies. He is a human being. The Nation of Islam teaches that one of the Gods, named Alfonso went into Europe and married a pure white woman and gave birth to a daughter, which was a mistake. The lesson says he, Alfonso(God) said, "Oops we missed that time." He wanted a son, so he tried again and they had a son. This son inherited the God-ship. He was half black and half white. The Nation of Islam knows this God(son of God) as W. Fard Muhammad. The Nation of Islam teaches that God manifested Himself in Fard Muhammad, a caucasian look-ing man. He came to North America to seek and to save the African-American people. This man Fard Muhammad, according to the teachings of the Nation of Islam, has the power to control the heavens and the earth, wind, hail, snow, and rain.

The God of the Nation of Islam is not an eternal being. He dies and his wisdom only lives "twenty-five thousand years." According to the Nation of Islam's teachings' the world is in the 25,000 year cycle of Fard Muhammad's wisdom. In fact, he is suppose to be the wisest and greatest God to have ever lived. He looks like a caucasian. His mother was a caucasian from the hills of Europe. According to Fard, there was another Black God, a scientist named Yakub. Yakub created the White man six thousand years ago.

As the reader can clearly see, the concept of God in the Religion of Al-Islam is extremely different than that of the Nation of Islam. Over one billion Muslims and others, believe and accept the concept of Allah(God) as it is presented in the Religion of Al-Islam and the Holy Quran. Only a few

5

thousand believe and accept the concept of God as it is presented by the Nation of Islam.

The Allah(God) of the Religion of Al-Islam, the Creator of the heavens and the earth is eternal. The entire creation is his kingdom. The god of the Nation of Islam is not eternal; his life is short-lived. In fact, I understand that the so-called leader of the Nation of Islam, Minister Farrakan, is attempting to change Fard Muhammad from God to Mahdi and replace Fard with the true Islamic concept of Allah(God). The concept of Allah in the Religion of Al-Islam can never be changed. Allah is bigger than everything. Nothing can contain Him. Fard Muhammad, the God of the Nation of Islam, a man, can be contained anywhere. The true God(Allah) never lived in Detroit, Chicago, New York, Oakland, California, Washington, D.C., Jerusalem or Mecca. He is over His entire creation.

CHAPTER THREE
THE MESSENGER OF ALLAH(GOD)

The Religion of Al-Islam: The Last Prophet and Messenger

Muslims, those who accept and practice the Religion of Al-Islam are required to believe in and accept all of the prophets and messengers from Adam to Muhammad. The Religion of Al-Islam teaches that prophet Muhammad Ibn Abdullah (Peace be upon Him) is the last prophet or Seal of the Prophets of Allah(God). Prophet Muhammad (PBUH) is the last messenger and the one to whom the Holy Quran was revealed. He was born in Mecca 570 AD and died in Medina. Over one billion people beleive and accept him as the last prophet.

Muslims in Africa, Asia, Europe, Arabia, America, India, and Russia declare that " there is no god but Allah and Prophet Muhammad" Ibn Abdullah is His last Messenger. In fact, it is a requirement for every perseon who calls himself a Muslim.

The Nation of Islam's Last Messenger

For over forty years, the Nation of Islam taught and preached that Elijah Muhammad was the last messenger of Allah. (See Message to the Blackman and Muhammmad Speaks Newspaper)   Elijah Muhammad was an African American who was born in Sandersville, GA in October, 1898. He died February 25, 1975. In 1975, his son Imam Warith Deen Mohammad became the leader. He made a lot of excellent and profound changes.   One of which was removing the false belief and teachings that his father Elijah Muhammad is/was the last Messenger of Allah(God). He successfully changed and directed the Nation of Islam to the universal teachings of the Religion of Al-Islam.

The majority of the members of the old Nation of Islam accepted the new direction. They are now real Muslims. IMAM W.D. Muhammad even changed the name of the

7

Nation of Islam to the World Community of Islam; and then to the American Muslim Mission. This was done in an effort to broaden the view and move the followers away from the old into the new. Imam W.D. Mohammad and his followers or supporters are members in the international community of muslims. They no longer are identified by an organizational name. They are Muslims.

After about two years Minister Farrakhan and other broke away and tried to rebuild the old Nation of Islam and its teachings. They continue to advocate the old teachings of the Nation of Islam. Minister Farrakhan continued to teach that Elijah Muhammad is the last messenger of Allah and not Prophet Muhammad Ibn Abdullah of Arabia. Minister Farrakhan picked up the old name "Nation of Islam." He rekindled the old teachings of the NOI. He rebuilt the Nation of Islam. For about three years the rebuilt NOI under the leadership of Minister Farrakhan taught that Elijah Muhammad was not dead but still alive physically. Farrakhan challenged the "Muhammad family" to dig up the grave and prove to him that Elijah Muhammad's body was in there. Some of Farrakhan's followers still believe and teach that Elijah Muhammad is physically alive. (see Final Call Newspaper October 1990 issue).

Although Minister Louis Farrakhan has declared on several occasions that "There is no god but Allah and Muhammad is His Messenger" and that he believes in Prophet Muhammad Ibn Abdullah and the Holy Quran, it still is not clear whether his followers believe that or not. I do know that some of them still believe that Elijah Muhammad is the last Messenger of Allah. On October 14, 1990 in Detroit Michigan, Minister Farrakhan told an audience of approximately twenty thousand people that Elijah Muhammad is his Divine leader, teacher and guide. He also said Elijah Muhammad is the man that he is trying to pattern his life after. His exact words were,"If I lived to be a thousand,

8

I could never thank Allah enough for raising up in our midst a divine leader, teacher and guide; the man who gave me the example that I am attempting to pattern my life after; the man who has made the Torah, the Gospel and the Quran relevant books for the struggle of our people for liberation and oppressed people throughout the world. I am speaking of none other than my leader teacher and guide, the most Honorable Elijah Muhammad."

The Religion of Al-Islam teaches that only Allah is Divine and that Prophet Muhammad Ibn Abdullah is the most excellent model and example for humanity. Muslims try to pattern themselves after the conduct of Prophet Muhammad Ibn Abdullah. The Holy Quran states,"Ye have indeed in the Apostle of Allah a beautiful pattern(of conduct) for any one whose hope is in Allah and the Final Day, and who engages much in the the praise of Allah."(Holy Quran 33:21)

CHAPTER FOUR
THE FINAL REVELATION

The Holy Quran: The Final Revelation

The Holy Quran is the rule and guide of every Muslim. Muslims accept and believe that the Holy Quran is the last revelation from Allah(God). Al-Islam teaches that the Holy Quran is a Divine book for all times. The Holy Quran was revealed to the last prophet and messenger, Muhammad Ibn Abdullah(PBUH). Muslims believe that the Holy Quran is the work of Allah(God) and it is the highest body of knowledge on this earth. The Holy Quran is a pure and perfect book. It is a summation and confirmation of all the previous holy books. The Religion of Al-Islam teaches that no other revelation will come to man. The Holy Quran is the last revelation. "Praise be to Allah Who hath sent to His servant the book and hath allowed therein no crookedness."(S18:A1)

What the Nation of Islam says about the Holy Quran

The Nation of Islam doesn't accept or teach that the Holy Quran was revealed by Allah(God) nor is it the last, final and complete revelation form Allah(God). The Nation of Islam teaches that the Holy Quran was written by men. According to the wisdom of the Nation fo Islam every 25,000 years, men (scientist) get together and write a Holy Book. The Nation of Islam also teaches that another Holy Book will come. For about fifty years it taught that the Holy Quran was to be used only for a certain period of time and then another book would be written in its place. (see Message to the Blackman p. 91,97)

In 1975, Imam W.D. Mohammad, the son of Elijah Muhammad changed the teachings concerning the Holy Quran. He told the members that the Holy Quran is the final revelation and that no other book was coming. In fact, W.D. Mohammad transformed the Nation of Islam into a totally new community. The majority of the members embraced the religion of Al-Islam. Minister Farrakhan, who calls himself the leader of the Nation of Islam, did not accept the changes and held on to the old teachings of the Nation of Islam. Imam W.D. Mohammad and the majority of the Muslims in America and the world are not members of the Nation of Islam, headed by Farrakhan. There are many things, concerning the Holy Quran, that is taught by the Nation of Islam that agree with the religion of Al-Islam's teachings of the Holy Quran. For example, Elijah Muhammad wrote in his book <u>Message to the Blackman</u>,"The Holy Quran Sharieff contains some of the most beautiful prayers that one ever heard read or recited. It is called the Glorious Quran and without mistake that is just what it is."(p. 92)

However, the Nation of Islam also teaches that the Holy Quran is not the last or final revelation, nor was it revealed to Prophet Muhammad(PBUH) by Allah. "There is another book that none has been able to see or read, its contents coming soon from Allah-the 'Last Book' which takes us into the Hereafter." Also,"The Holy Quran, the Glory Books, should be read and studied by us, the so-called American Negroes. Both the present Bible and the Holy Quran must soon give way to that Holy Book which no man as yet but Allah has seen." And "We, the original nation of the earth...are the writers of the Bible and Quran. We make such history once every 25,000 years. When such history is written, it is done by twenty-four of our scientists. One acts as Judge or God for the others and twenty-three actually do the work of getting up the future of the nation, and all is put into one book and at intervals where such and such part or portion will come to pass, that people will be given that part of the book through one among that people from one of the twelve(twelve major scientists) as it is then called a Scripture which actually means script of writing from something original or book." (<u>Message to the Blackman</u>, p. 108)

11

CHAPTER FIVE
THE CONCEPT OF MAN

The Religion of Al-Islam: Concept of Man

The Holy Quran says Allah(God) created man with a good nature. Allah created the human "in the best mold." Every human being is created in nobility. According to the Religion of Al-Islam every human being has a natural inclination towards good, righteousness, and truth. Man is intrusted with the role of leader in creation. Allah gave man a limited free will and he can decide which road he wants to travel in life. The Holy Quran also says Allah(God) gave the human being the gift of knowledge. Man was given the knowledge of creation.(S2:A31)   The human being was created and raised above the angels(forces in nature).

According to Al-Islam every human is created by one God, Allah, the most high. There is no superiority of a black over a white or a white over a black, or and Arab over a non-Arab etc. stated prophet Muhammad Ibn Abdullah(PBUH) in his farewell address. Al-Islam teaches that all humans have the same potential for progress. The Prophet Muhammad (PBUH) said,"Every person is born a Muslim." Any human being can become a muslim. Al-Islam is not just for a particular group of people. Man is created perfect in his nature. Al-Islam makes a clear distinction between (God) Allah and man. Allah is all powerful and independent. Man is totally dependent on Allah for everything.   However Allah(God) has given us the freedom to think and reason. Allah has blessed the human being with intelligence. The Holy Quran says man is created to worship Allah(God). "Nay but worship Allah(God) and be of those who give thanks." (S39:A66)

The Nation of Islam's Concept of Man

The Nation of Islam's idea of a man is quite different from that of Al-Islam. The Nation of Islam teaches that there are two totally different human beings with extremely

12

different natures.

The Blackman and the caucasian, white man. According to the Nation of Islam's teachings' the Blackman is the Original man, the owner, the maker, the cream of the planet earth, god of the universe. The Blackman is god. His nature is righteous. In the book <u>Message to the Blackman</u>, it reads, "The Original man, Allah has declared, is none other than the Blackman. The Blackman is the first and last, maker and owner of the universe. From him came all brown, yellow, red and white people." (p.53) The Holy Quran, the book that is accepted as the last revelation from Allah, by over one billion Muslims clearly states that Allah (God) is the Owner and Maker of the universe, not man. It states, "It is He who created the heavens and the earth in true (portion)." (39:5) The Holy Quran also states, "Blessed is He who made constellations in the skies, and place therein a lamp and a moon giving light; and it is He who made the night and day to follow each other." (S25:A61 & 62) The Holy Quran clearly states that man is created by Allah (God). It reads, "Allah Most Gracious! It is He who has taught the Quran. He has created man: He taught him speech (and intelligence)." (S55:A1-4)

The Nation of Islam teaches something totally different from the Holy Quran and the Religion of Al-Islam. Not only does it (NOI) teach that there are two different types of human beings; It also teaches that they (Black and White people) were created and made by different Gods. It teaches that the Blackman is self-created. the White man was made by a Blackman named Yakub, 6,000 years ago. Yakub taught the caucasian, White man wickedness. He also taught them how to rule the Blackman. (see <u>Message to the Blackman</u>, p. 103-122).

The Nation of Islam teaches that man is God. Man can evolve to such a high mental level until he becomes God.

13

"God is a man and we just cannot make Him other than man, lest we make Him an inferior one; for man's intelligence has no equal in other than man. His wisdom is infinite; capable of accomplishing anything that His brain can conceive...Let that one among you who believe God is other than man prove it!"(Message to the Blackman, p. 6,7)

The Holy Quran says that the disbelievers during Moses' time said similar things. "And remember ye said 'O Moses! We shall never believe in thee until we see Allah (God) manifestly..."(S2:A55)

CHAPTER SIX
THE FUNDAMENTAL PRINCIPLES OF AL-ISLAM

Fundamental Principles of Al-Islam

As Muslims, we are to have a universal and holistic view of man and the world. Al-Islam is a comprehensive religion, in that it addresses every aspect of human life. The human being, as mentioned earlier, begins his growth through the five senses, which are very important. They, in many ways, serve as a foundation from which we support ourselves. Our religion (Al-Islam) consists of five basic, but essential principles, namely:

> 1. To bear witness that there is no god except One Allah(God), the Eternal and Absolute; and that Prophet Muhammad Ibn Abdullah is His last Prophet and Messenger.
>
> 2. To make Prayer five times a day.
>
> 3. To pay Charity.
>
> 4. To Fast during the month of Ramadan.
>
> 5. To make Hajj(Pilgrimage) to the Holy House in Makkah(once in a lifetime).

It is reported that one day while Prophet Muhammad (PBUH) was sitting with some of the believers and companions, there appeared before them a man whose clothes were "exceedingly white and whose hair was exceedingly black." He walked up and sat by the Prophet Muhammad (PBUH) placing his knees against the Prophet's knees, with his hand on his thigh and said,"O Muhammad, tell me about Al-Islam." The Prophet said," Islam is to testify that there is no god but Allah, and Muhammad is the Messenger of Allah; to perform the prayers; to pay the Zakat(charity); to Fast in the month of Ramadan; and to make the Pil-

15

grimage to the House (Ka'aba) if you are able to do so." He said,"You have spoken rightly!"(Forty Hadith)

What the Muslims Believe

As Muslims, we also have six fundamentals beliefs, called "Articles of Faith." They are:

1. Belief in the Oneness of Allah(H.Q.112)

2. Belief in all of the Prophets(3:84)

3. Belief in all the revealed books (4:136)

4. Belief in the Angels(2:177)

5. Belief in the Hereafter and Judgement (2:4)

6. Belief in Divine Ordinance or Pre-Detemination (47:22)

Allah tells us in Al-Quran that we must believe in these Articles of Faith and conduct ourselves accordingly. "... Whoso disbelieve in Allah, and His angels, and His Scriptures, and His Messengers, and the Last Day, he verily has wandered far astray."(H.Q. 4:136)

We should study these principles or articles so that we can better understand them. The study of these principles is called Aqidah.

What the Nation of Islam Believes

The following information can be found in the book Our Savior Has Arrived(p. 223) or any Muhammad Speaks or Final Call Newspaper. It is incorrectly titled "What the Muslims Believe."

1. We Believe in the One God Whose proper Name is Allah.

2. We Believe in the Holy Quran and in the Scriptures of all the Prophets of God.

3. We Believe in the truth of the Bible but we believe that it has been tampered with and must be reinter preted so that mankind will not be snared by the falsehoods that have been added to it.

4. We Believe in Allah's Prophets and the Scriptures they brought to the people.

5. We Believe in the resurrection of the dead-not in physical resurrection-but in mental resurrection. We Believe that the so-called Negroes are most in need of mental ressurection: therefore, they will be resurrected first.

Furthermore, we believe we are the people of God's choice, as it has been written, that God would choose the rejected and the despised. We can find no other persons fitting this description in these last days more than the so-called Negroes in America. We believe in the resurrection of the righteous.

6. We Believe in the judgement; we believe this first judgement will take place as God revealed, in America...

7. We Believe this is the time in history for the seperation of the so-called Negroes and the so-called white Americans. We believe the black man should be freed in name as well as in fact. By this we mean that he should be freed from the names imposed upon him by his former slave masters. Names that

identified him as being the slave master's slave. We believe that if we are free indeed, we should go in our own people's name-the black peoples on earth.

8. We Believe in justice for all, whether in God or not; we believe as others, that we are due equal justice as human beings. We believe in equality-as a nation-of equals. We do not believe that we are equal with our slave masters in the status of freed "slaves."

We recognize and respect American citizens as inde pendent peoples and we respect their laws which govern this nation.

9. We Believe that the offer of integration is hypocriti cal and is made by those who are trying to deceive the black peoples into believing that their 400 year old enemies of freedom, justice and equality are, all of a sudden, their friends. Furthermore, we believe that such deception is intended to prevent black people from realizing that the time in history has arrived for the separation from the whites of this nation.

If the white people are truthful about their professed friendship toward the so-called Negro, they can prove it by dividing up America with their slaves. We do not believe that America will ever be able to furnish enough jobs for her own millions of unem ployed, in addition to jobs for the 20,000,000 black people as well.

10. We Believe that we who declared ourselves to be righteous Muslims, should not participate in wars which take the lives of humans. We do not believe this nation should force us to take part in such wars, for we have nothing to gain from it unless America agrees to give us the necessary territory wherein we

may have something to fight for.

11. We Believe our woman should be respected and protected as the woman of other nationalities are respected and protected.

12. We Believe that Allah(God) appeared in the Person of Master W. Fard Muhammad, July, 1930; the long-awaited "Messiah" of the Christians and "Mahdi" of the Muslims. We believe further and lastly that Allah is God and besides Him there is no God and He will bring about a universal government of peace wherein we all can live in peace together.

CHAPTER SEVEN
THE HEREAFTER

What the Religion of Al-Islam Says about the Hereafter or Life After Death

Belief in the hereafter is an essential part of Muslim life. The Religion of Al-Islam teaches that every human being will be raised from the dead to account for his actions in this physical world. Belief in the Hereafter is one of the Articles of Faith. The Holy Quran tells us that Allah can bring about a total resurrection of any human being. The Quran also tells us that the unbelievers asked, "What when we die and become dust shall we live again?" There has always been those who doubted and disbelieved in life after death or the hereafter and Resurrection. Muslims must accept the idea of life after death, it is a vital component of the Religion of Al-Islam, as well as an intelligent belief. We all will be compensated for our intentions and deeds. The Holy Quran gives the following statements, comments and ideas about the hereafter:

Were we then weary with the first creation, That they should be in confused doubt about a new creation? (H.Q.50:15)

And they(sometimes) say,"There is nothing except our life on this earth, and never shall we be raised up again." (H.Q.6:29)

What is the life of this world but play and amusement? But best is the home in the Hereafter, for those who are righteous. Will ye not then understand?(H.Q.6:32)

Those who listen in (truth), Be sure, will accept: As to the dead, Allah will raise them up then will they be turned unto Him.(H.Q. 6:36)

And they say,"What is there but our life in this world? We shall die and we live, and nothing but time can destroy us." But that they have no knowledge: They merely conjecture: And when Our clear signs are rehearsed to them, their argument is nothing but this: they say,"Bring (back) our forefathers, if what ye say is true!" Say,"It is Allah who gives life, then gives you death; then He will gather you together for the Day of Judgement about which there is no doubt," But most men do not understand.(H.Q.45:24-6)

"What! When we die and become dust, (shall we live again?) That is a (sort of) return far (from our understanding)" We already know how much of them the earth takes away: with Us is a record guarding (the full account). But they deny the truth when it comes to them: So they are in a confused state. (H.Q.50:3-5)

They swear their strongest oaths by God, that God will not raise up those who die: Nay, but it is a promise(binding) on Him in truth: But most among mankind realize it not. (H.Q.16:38)

They say,"What! When we are reduced to bones and dust, should we really be raised up (to be) a new creation?" Say,"(Nay!) be ye stones or iron, or created matter, which in your minds is hardest(to be raised up, yet shall ye be raised up)!" Then will they say,"Who will cause us to return?" Say,"He Who created you first!" (H.Q. 17:49-51)

Man says,"What! When I am dead, shall I then be raised up alive?" But does not man call to mind that We created him before out of nothing? (H.Q. 19:66-7)

Does man think that We cannot assemble his bones? Nay, we are able to put together in perfect order the very tips of his fingers. (H.Q.75:3-4)

The Nation of Islam's Concept of the Hereafter and Life After Death

"We Believe in the resurrection of the dead-not in physical resurrection-but in mental resurrection..."
(The Muslim Program: What the Muslims Believe-see old Muhammad Speaks or Final Call newspapers)

The Nation of Islam teaches that the only Hereafter, is on this earth after the destruction of the evil, wicked white race. The Nation of Islam does not teach that there will be a spiritual resurrection and that Allah can and may bring about a physical resurrection from the dead. In the book The Supreme Wisdom, Elijah Muhammad writes, "My people have been deceived by the arch deceiver in regards to the Hereafter. They think the Hereafter is a life of spirits(spooks) up somewhere in the sky, while it is only on earth, and you won't change to any spirit beings. The life in the Hereafter is only a continuation of the present life. You will be flesh and blood. You won't see spooks coming up out of graves to meet God."(p. 26)

In the book, Message to the Blackman, it reads "No already physically dead person will be in the Hereafter; that is slavery belief, taught to slaves to keep them under control. This is taught also so that they won't be thinking about the wealth of their slave-masters while under the slave-master.

The slave is made to believe his will come after death, and his master knows that death settles all, and that you can't return to tell him whether he lied or told the truth...There is no such thing as dying and coming up out of the earth, meeting your friends and meeting those who died before you...When you are dead, you are dead."
(p. 168, 304)

The Holy Quran says, They swear their strongest oaths by Allah, that Allah will not raise up those who die: "Nay, but it is a promise(binding) on Him in truth: But most among mankind realize it not." (H.Q. 16:38)

The book Supreme Wisdom states,"You who believe literally in the physical resurrection of the dead, must remember the Bible(Rev. 14:4) teaches that the first righteous to be saved (the 144,000) are redeemable from among men, not out of the grave...Surely there is a resurrection of the dead. It is one of the principles of Al-Islam, but not the physically dead in the graveyards. It is the mentally dead, the ignorant, whom the devil's false-hood has killed to the knowledge of truth... You and I know that it can't refer to a physically dead person, because that one won't and can't rise again. What is left to rise from a body that has gone back to the earth or up in smoke or eaten by some wild beast or fish of the sea? What about the people who died before the flood and after. Even Adam? They have nothing to rise from." (p. 35-6)

Now let us turn our attention to the Belief in the Judgement.

CHAPTER EIGHT
THE JUDGEMENT

The Judgement

Muslims believe in the Day of Judgement. We believe that one day Allah (God) will destroy this whole creation and each individual will have to stand before Allah (God) and be granted paradise or hell- fire. The Holy Quran says, "One day we shall remove the mountains, and thou will see the earth as a level stretch, and We shall gather them all together, nor shall We leave out any one of them. And they will be marshalled before thy Lord in ranks (with the announcement), 'Now have ye come to Us (Bare) as We created you first: aye, ye thought We shall not fulfill the appointment made to you to meet (Us).' And the book (of deeds) will be placed (before you)..." (H.Q. 18:47-9)

Allah also says in the Holy Quran, "Verily, we have warned you of a Penalty near - The Day when man will see (the deeds) which his hands have sent forth, and the Unbelievers will say, 'Woe unto me! Would that I were (mere) dust!" (H.Q. 78:40)

Man is essentially a composite of physical, mental and spiritual. The Creator, Allah, created every aspect of the human being, therefore He can destroy and resurrect every aspect or element of the human being. Allah will show us exactly what we have done in this life. He will change the entire creation on the Day of Judgement. The Holy Quran says, "When the sky is cleft asunder; When the stars are scattered; When the oceans are suffered to burst forth; and when the graves are turned upside down; Then shall each soul know what it hath sent forward and (what it hath) kept back." (H.Q. 82:1-5)

The Holy Quran, the final authority in the Muslim's life, assures us that there will be a Day of Judgement and it explains how and what will happen. "Verily the Day of Sorting out is a thing appointed;The Day that the

Trumpet shall be sounded, and ye shall come forth in crowds; and the heavens shall be opened as if there were doors, and the mountains shall vanish, as if they were a mirage." (H.Q. 78:17-20)

What the Nation of Islam Says About the Judgement

The Nation of Islam teaches that the Judgement will first take place in America and that it will be carried out, by a space ship called the Mother Plane. It teaches that this Circular Plane will save the African American people from the Caucasians. It will take us (African Americans) up into space(out of the earth's atmosphere) for about a thousand years. Meanwhile, smaller planes will drop bombs on the earth. These bombs will go a mile deep and blow up mountains a mile high. In the section entitled,"What The Muslims Believe, it states,"We believe in the judgement; we believe this first judgement will take place, as God revealed, in America." We also find written in the book Message to the Blackman under the sub heading "Battle in the Sky is Near,""The Great Wheel which many of us see in the sky today is not so much a wheel as one may think in such terms, but rather a place made like a wheel . The like of this wheel-like plane was never seen before. Throughout the Bible and Holy Quran teachings on the judgement and destruction of the enemies, fire will be used as the last weapon."

"The present wheel-shaped plane known as the Mother of Planes, is one-half mile by a half mile and it is the largest mechanical man-made object in the sky. It is a small human planet made for the purpose of destroying the present world of the enemies of Allah.

The cost to build such a plane is staggering! The finest brains were used to build it. It is capable of staying in outer space six to twelve months at a time without

25

coming into the earth's gravity. It carried fifteen hundred bombing planes with the most deadliest explosives-the type used in bringing up mountains on the earth. The very same method is to be used in the destruction of this world.

The bombs are equipped with motors and the toughest of steel was used in making them. This steel drills and takes the bombs into the earth at a depth of one mile and is timed not to explode until it reaches one mile into the earth. This explosion produces a mountain one mile high; not one bomb will fall into water. They will all fall on cities. The small circular-made planes called flying saucers, which are so much talked of being seen, could be from this Mother Plane. This is only one of the things in store for the white man's evil world. Believe it or believe it not!"

Minister Farrakhan, the leader of the Nation of Islam has often said that he had a vision that he was on this Mother Plane and there he saw Elijah Muhammad, the former leader of the Nation of Islam; who has been dead now for 15 years. Minister Farrakhan says that Elijah Muhammad warned him that America was going to bomb Libya.

The Religion of Al-Islam does not teach that the judgement will be brought about by a flying saucer or Mother Ship. It teaches that Allah will destroy the wicked and save the righteous.

Allah does not need bombs and planes etc. He only says, "Be and it is."

The Holy Quran says,"And our command is but a single (act) like the twinkling of an eye."(H.Q. 54:50)

26

CHAPTER NINE
THE CONCEPT OF SATAN

The Concept of Satan

The Religion of Al-Islam does not teach that one group of people are "a race of devils." Muslims are required to seek refuge in Allah from the rejected, Satan: each time we read the Holy Quran or stand for prayer. The Muslim from Africa must seek refuge from Satan, the Muslim from Europe, Asia, Arabia, America, Turkey, Russia, Jerusalem, Iran etc., all must seek refuge in Allah from Satan. Satan's influence has been felt in each part of the earth. The Holy Quran says Satan, the devil told Allah that he was going to attack the human being from before him, behind him, from the left and the right. He (Satan) said he would even lay and wait on the straight path. "I will lie in wait for them on Thy Straight Way: Then will I assault them from their right and their left" Nor wilt Thou find in most of them, gratitude (for thy mercies)." (H.Q.7:16 & 7)

Satan is wise enough to take on different colors and to appear in different nationalities. The Religion of Al-Islam teaches that Satan (know as Iblis) was originally a Jinn that was the leader among the angels. He was a creature of light and fire. But he rebelled against the command of Allah. This reduced him to the level of Satan, the rejected one. The Holy Quran says he became proud and arrogant. He refused to submit to the man that Allah (God) made. "Behold We said to the angels, "Bow down to Adam." And they bowed down: Not so Iblis: he refused and was haughty: he was of those who reject faith." (H.Q.2:34) This evil and rebellious spirit can dominate any human being. We as human beings can take on a devil mentality. History shows us that someone from every race or nationality has taken on a devil mentality at one point and caused death and destruction in the lives of people.

The Nation of Islam's Concept of Satan

Just as the Nation of Islam teaches that God is a man, it also teaches that Satan, the devil is a man. The Caucasian, white man. The Nation of Islam teaches that the White man is the Devil and is evil by nature. He is a grafted man. He is the Satan of the Bible and the Holy Quran, says the Nation of Islam. Fard Muhammad taught Elijah Muhammad and his followers that the Caucasian, White man is 100% evil and they will never accept the religion of Al-Islam. "The White race, by nature, can't be righteous. Islam was taught to them from Moses to Muhammad, but they were never able to live the life of a Muslim believer and can't do it today." (Supreme Wisdom, p. 30)

According to the wisdom of Fard Muhammad, the founder of the Nation of Islam, Satan, the Devil was made by a Black man named Yakub, somewhere called "Pelan." According to the teachings of the Nation of Islam,"The Yakub made devils were really pale white, with really blue eyes; which we think are the ugliest of colors for a human eye. They were called caucasian-which means, according to some of the Arab scholars, 'One whose evil effect is not confined to one's self alone, but affects others.' After Yakub made the White race, he taught them how to lie, steal, murder and rule the Black race. (see Message to the Blackman: The Making of the Devil, p. 103-22).

28

CHAPTER TEN
THE DRESS CODE

The Religion of Al-Islam: Dress Code

The Religion of Al-Islam encourages modesty. Muslims are required to be conscious of their dress. They should not expose parts of their body to the public that Allah mentions in the Holy Quran. Because Al-Islam is a universal religion, there is no particular uniform that each Muslim must wear in his or her daily life. Allah says in the Holy Quran that the "garments of righteousness" are the best.

> O ye children of Adam! We have bestowed raiment upon you to cover your shame, as well as to be an adornment to you. But the raiment of righteousness, that is the best...(S7:A26)

> And say to the believing women that they should lower their gaze and guard their modesty; that they should not display their beauty and ornaments except what (must ordinarily) appear thereof; that they should draw their veils over their bosoms and not display their beauty...(S24:A31)

Nation of Islam's Dress Code

The members of the Nation of Islam, especially the men are easily recognized by their style of dress. Usually a suit, white shirt and bow tie; close cut hair style and clean face (no facial hair). They also wear blue and red FOI uniform. They are also encouraged to keep themselves clean and decent.

The women are taught that they should cover their hair and wear long dresses and never to expose their body in public.

CHAPTER ELEVEN
RAMADAN(FASTING)

Those who practice the religion of Al-Islam, Muslims, are obligated to fast during the Holy month of Ramadan. This is the month in which the Holy Quran was revealed to Prophet Muhammad Ibn Abdullah(PBUH). Because the Muslim world uses the lunar calendar, this month rotates through all four seasons.   During the month of Ramadan, Muslims abstain from food, drink, sex etc.., during the daylight hours. However, during the night, the Muslims are allowed to eat, drink and have sex with their wives etc.   Muslims are encouraged to make extra prayers and to read the entire Holy Quran during the Month of Ramadan.   Muslims are encouraged to be more peaceful and tolerant of themselves and others.

The Holy Quran says concerning Ramadan,"O ye who believe!   Fasting is prescribed to you as it was prescribed to those before you, that ye may (learn) self-restraint..."

Ramadan is the (month) in which was sent down the Quran, as a guide to mankind also clear(signs) for guidance and judgement(Between right and wrong).   So every one of you who is present (at his home) during that month should spend it in fasting, but if any one is ill, or on a journey, the prescribed period(should be made up)by days later. Allah intends every facility for you;   He does not want to put you to difficulties.   (He wants you) to complete the prescribed period, and to glorify Him in that He has guided you;   and perchance ye shall be grateful."(S2:A183-5)

The Nation of Islam: Fasting

The members of the Nation of Islam fast in the

30

month of December as a protest to the Christian Holiday, Christmas. As a general rule they don't fast along with the broader Muslim community. Nowadays, it is an option for the members of the Nation of Islam to fast or not to fast during the Holy month of Ramadan.

In the book How to Eat to Live, by Elijah Muhammad, it states,"I prescribe for you the month of December to fast in-if you are able to take the fast-instead of the regular month that travels through the year, called Ramadan by the Muslims; the month in which they say Muhammad received the Holy Quran. Why did I prescribe for you the month of December? It is because it was in this month that you used to worship a dead prophet by the name of Jesus. And it was the month that you wasted your money and wealth to worship the 25th day of this month, December, as the Christians do." (p. 48)

The Nation of Islam fast during a totally different time and for a totally different reason than those state in the Holy Quran, the final authority for Muslims.

CHAPTER TWELVE
SALAT PRAYER

The Religion of Al-Islam: Prayer

Prayer is one of the most important pillars in Al-Islam. It is an essential activity for Muslim life. Muslims perform prayer (salat) five times a day, every day of the year. The Muslim prayer consists of several movements from standing to bowing to kneeling. They are called Qiyam, Ruku, Jalsa, and Sajda.

Muslims must perform prayer in this manner, as long as he/she is physically able to do so.

The Holy Quran says: And establish regular prayers at the two ends of the day and at the approaches of the night: For those things that are good remove those that are evil. (11:114) "Enjoin prayer on thy people and be constant therein..." (S20:A132)

Muslims are obligated to establish regular prayer. Prayer purifies the mind and spirit. Prayer is a physical activity and it gives us spiritual discipline.

The Nation of Islam: And Prayer

Members of the Nation of Islam are also encouraged to pray. However, they are not encouraged to establish Salat. I am sure some of them do perform salat as the religion of Al-Islam requires, however that is not one of its (NOI) trademarks. The knowledge of salat is available to the members of the Nation of Islam. The importance of prayer is emphasized in the book "Message to the Blackman: Surely the best way to strive to be upright in a sinful world is to pray continuously to the one true God, whose proper name is Allah for guidance...Prayer is obligatory in Islam." It also states, "We must study the words and different positions taken by the Muslim in his daily prayer. This helps us to understand better the true way to worship Allah(God)."(p. 139)   As a whole the members of the Nation of Islam don't make salat. They only make duas. In some places the members of the NOI do perform Jumah prayer (Friday community prayer) and in other places they don't.

The Islamic Mosque(Masjid)

According to the religion of Islam, the mosque must be structured and built on taqwa(loving fear for Allah). The purpose is to worship Allah. The mosque is to be built soley for the pleasure of Allah(God).   Muslims come to the mosque for prayer and study. In most Islamic countries the mosque is open all day and night for the five daily prayers. Muslims enter the mosque without going through any physical checking procedure by security guards. The mosque is open to all people. Friday is the day when all Muslims are required to attend the mosque for Jumah(congregational prayer) Before the prayer). the Imam gives a two part lecture based on the Holy Quran and Sunnah of Prophet Muhammad.

The Nation of Islam's house of worship is quite different.

The Nation of Islam's Temple

In order for someone to enter the Nation of Islam's temple or house of worship, he/she must accept to be physically checked and searched by security guards called FOI. The doors of the NOI are closed to caucasians. Anyone cannot just walk into the temple and make prayer. Generally, there is no place for salat in the temple. Temple meetings are held on Sunday, Wednesday and Friday for the general public. Saturday is reserved for FOI class. In a few places throughout the USA the temples are open for Jumah prayer, and some of them(Temples) are called mosque. However, that is the exception and not the rule.

Islamic Observance Days

Those who practice the Religion of Al-Islam, observe two Holidays. They are called 'Idul-Fitr and 'Idul-Adha.

'Idul-Fitr, the Festival of Fastbreaking is celebrated on the first of the lunar month of Shawwal. This religious festival in fact is an expression of Thanksgiving to Allah for His grace in enabling His faithful servants to observe the month of Ramadan. 'Idul-Fitr marks the end of Ramadan, announcing that the Fast is over and that the Zakat must be paid . The charity called Saadaqa-Fitr is binding on every Muslim that can afford it. Men are required to pay the charity on behalf of themselves, their wives and children. It is obligatory to pay this charity prior to the 'Idul-Fitr prayer.

'Idul-Adha is celebrated on the 10th of the lunar month of Zil-Hajj commemorating the great sacrifice offered by Prophets Abraham and Isma'il (Allah's peace be upon them both). By slaughtering the sacrificial animals, Muslims pledge before Allah that just as they are shedding their blood for His sake, so will they be able and ready to lay down their own lives for the sake/ cause of Allah.

Nation of Islam's Observance Days

The major Observance or Holiday for the Nation of Islam is celebrated on February 26. On this day, they have a national meeting each year to celebrate the birthday of Fard Muhammad. It is believed that he was born on February 26, 1877.

In the last few years, however, Minister Farrakhan has changed this observance day to October 7, in celebration of Elijah Muhammad. Some of his followers observe both days. These days are called "Savior's Day."

CHAPTER THIRTEEN
THINGS TO CONSIDER

Things to Consider

Before concluding, we would like to leave our reader with a few things to reflect upon. First of all, the Religion of Al-Islam is and has been a positive force in the life of man and it has not yet been given due and proper exposure. The Religion of Al-Islam is studied secretly by some caucasians in America and these people know the value and power of Al-Islam. Some of them don't want it to flourish among the masses. I suggest that the reader at least attempt to find out as much about the Religion of Al-Islam as possible.

On the other hand, for those who are interested in the Nation of Islam, I simply say this, it is not all that it appears to be. If one looks beyond the surface of the NOI and look deeper into its teachings, he/she will find a shallow grave. In that grave you will find a dead man that wants to be raised by the Religion of Al-Islam. History clearly shows that the Religion of Al-Islam has that attracting power necessary to raise human beings from mental, moral and spiritual death. It has the power to make man productive and enlightened.

Al-Islam gives us a sober message. The people need to know the truth about the Religion of Al-Islam. Al-Islam doesn't condemn the Blackman or any other man for crimes that have been committed by others. It doesn't tell us that we are naturally wicked and evil. The Religion of Al-Islam doesn't tell us that the Blackman is the source of evil and wickedness. Nor does it tell the world that the Chief devil, the Father of the devil is the Blackman and that we are therefore responsible for all the corruption, lies and deceit and murder that is being committed in the world by the caucasian whiteman .

On the other hand however, the Nation of Islam does teach that the Blackman is the source of evil. It also teaches that the Blackman is God and is by nature righteous; However, it also puts the whiteman's wickedness and evil on the Blackman. We are blamed for the devil being on earth. This is what Fard Muhammad taught Elijah Muhammad who in turn taught his followers. (Read the book Message to the Blackman, p. 103-22). Fard Muhammad said that a Blackman name Yakub made the Devil about 6000 years ago through a process of grafting. The devil, who he said is the whiteman, was not only made physically by the Blackman but was also taught how to be evil and wicked by the Blackman. Fard Muhammad a foreigner not an African American, taught African Americans that one of our people taught the Whiteman how to lie, steal, murder and deceive Black people. He said we (Black people) made the White people devils.

Black People Did Not Make the Devil

Ever since we have been here in America racist caucasians and others have always presented us to the world as an evil useless violent prone criminal minded people. For hundreds of years the christian church taught that we were cursed black because one of our people, Ham, looked at his father's nakedness and laughed. The world has been taught that the Devil in hell, the Satan is Black and that evil is of the dark or black side of nature. In the media, they present African Americans in a negative light. The TV shows depict the bad guy in black. In the Western world death is associated with black. What Fard Muhammad said about us making the devil, one of our own being the Father of the devil and the chief master mind in teaching White

37

people how to be evil, doesn't sound any different than what the white racist of the north and south have said about African Americans.

Black people are not responsible for the crimes of caucasians or any one else. In recent years we have been the victims of racism and false unnatural teachings. We have followed the footsteps of the Caucasian whiteman.

Believe me, the whiteman don't/didn't need the Blackman to teach him how to lie, steal, murder and deceive anyone. The whiteman is capable and have always been capable of being wicked and evil without the help of the Blackman or any other man. In fact, they are better equipped to teach themselves how to lie, steal and murder than any Blackman can teach them. Before the Whiteman ever saw a Blackman they(Caucasians) were killing and slaughtering each other like wild beast. Who taught them that? Not us.

History teaches us that the caucasians, before they had contact with the Blacks of Africa and before they came into the light of civilization, were cannibals. History also reveals that they had some of the worst wars among themselves then any other people. If you read about the Vikings and the Huns and other caucasian tribes, you will see that they never needed Black people to teach them how to murder; if anything they needed someone to teach them how to be civilized. We should reject any notion or suggestion that Black people made the Devil (White people) and taught them how to be wicked and evil.

The Religion of Al-Islam teaches that all human beings are created in nobility and excellence. It teaches that man can evolve and grow to the level of a perfect human being. The Religion of Al-Islam does not lash out against any race or group of people. It lashes out against injustice, racism, oppression and ignorance, evil and wickedness. The Religion of Al-Islam, if practiced correctly, brings about a peaceful co-existence between man and man.

Conclusion

The Religion of Al-Islam is for all people. The Honorable Elijah Muhammad knew that, as he grew older and wiser. He wanted and hoped that his people would accept and embrace the universal teachings of Al-Islam. He wanted his followers to evolve up out of the teachings of the Nation of Islam into the vast and perfect teachings of the Religion of Al-Islam. He worked hard to prepare his followers for that day. In fact, he knew it would happen. In 1974, the year his son Wallace D. Muhammad returned to the NOI, Elijah Muhammad wrote and published the book - Our Savior Has Arrived. A year later his son became the leader of the NOI. Elijah knew it was time. If you read that book you will find some of the instructions or advice that he left concerning the steps that should be taken in order to bring about the necessary changes. Elijah Muhammad said, "The first way to bring about something new is to change the way of thinking of the people. When you have removed from the people the old mind and idea then you can insert new ideas into their minds." (p.121,122) That is exactly what his son Wallace D. Muhammad did. He said, "MAN MEANS MIND!" He created a new word environment; and the followers took on a new mind. However, others wanted to hold onto the old mind. That is why you still have an organization calling itself the Nation of Islam, and a man calling himself the leader of the NOI.

The Honorable Elijah Muhammad did a great work for his people and is one of the greatest social reformers of our time. He should be respected and honored for his excellent work among African Americans. Although as Muslims, we must reject the teachings of his teacher Fard Muhammad, we should still respect and love the work that Elijah Muhammad did that was positive in the life of so many people. We should also be reminded that another great leader by the name of Malcolm X; Al-hajj Malik Shabazz was a Muslim and he evolved through the narrow teachings of the NOI into the universal teachings of the Religion of Al-Islam. He practiced Al-Islam.

Now is the time for all of those who follow the old teachings of the NOI to make the change and began practicing the Religion of Al-Islam with all other Muslims. The difference between the teachings and beliefs of the Religion of Islam and the Nation of Islam are very clear. Perhaps one day those differences will fade away and the members of the NOI will come to understand the real importance of following the teachings of the Holy Quran and the sunnah of Prophet Muhammad, the last prophet of Allah. Perhaps they will have the strength to immediately begin practicing the Religion of Al-Islam. However, even if they don't, we must continue to do our part in teaching the Religion of Al-Islam to the people. You the reader, I hope that you have at least been able to learn the difference between the teachings of the Religion of Al-Islam and the Nation of Islam. If you have learned that, then I have achieved my purpose.

O ye who believe!
Persevere in patience
And constancy; vie
in such perseverance;
Strengthen each other;
And fear Allah (God);

Comments

Any comments concerning this book or any book written by the author, Mustafa El-Amin should be sent to the following address.

P.O. Box 32148
Newark, NJ 07102

FOOD FOR THOUGHT

"The ink of the scholar is more Holy
than the blood of the martyr"

"He who leaveth home in search of
knowledge, walketh in the path of
God." - Prophet Muhammad

"Reflect before you speak; you will
so avoid error"
"One who reflects on God's gifts,
succeeds"

"Ignorance works a man more harm
than a cancer in the body"

"If you aren't a brilliant and learned
talker, be an attentive listener'

"Either lead, follow or get out of
the way"

"The wisest is he who does not disdain
the nature of the man"

"Greed is permanent slavery"

"The color of a man doesn't change
the nature of the man"

"The fools only see the external, wise
men see both the external and internal"

"The strongest man is whoever can make
his reason conquer his passion"

"The believer is one with whom people's
life, wealth and dignity are secure"

"The believer is not proud or selfish,
he does not degrade nor backbite"

"The Fool sees naught but folly; and
the mad man only madness. Yesterday
I asked a foolish man to count the
fools among us. He laughed and said,
"This is too hard a thing to do, and
it will take too long. Were it not
better to count only the wise'?"

"God has given you knowledge, so that by
its light you may not only worship him,
but also see yourself from in your weakness
and strength" - Kahill Gibran

"Oh you who believe, die not except in
a state of Islam (submission)." - Holy
Quran

"Those who believe (in the Quran) And
those who follow the Jewish (scriptures),
And the Christians and Sabians, And
who believe in God And the Last Day, And
work righteousness Shall have their re-
ward with their Lord, on them shall be no
fear, nor shall they grieve" - (Holy Quran)

SUGGESTED READINGS

1. Holy Quran, A. Yusuf Ali Translation

2. Prayer and Al-Islam, Imam W.D Muhammad
   Muhammad Islamic Foundation
   Chicago, Illinoins, 1982

3. An African American Genesis, Imam W.D. Moham
   med
   M.A.C.A. Publications,
   Calumet City, Illinois, 1986

4. Muhammad Encyclopedia of Seerah, Vol. 1,
   Affzal Ur Rahman, the Muslim School TRUST,
   London England, 1981

5. The Life of Muhammad, Haykal
   American Trust Publications

6. Prophet Muhammad: The Human Model,
   Abdul-Kabir Shamsiddeen, New Mind Productions
   1990

7. INTRODUCTION TO ISLAM, Dr. M. Hamidullah
   Kazi Publications 1981

8. Al-Islam, Christianity and Freemasonry,
   Mustafa El-Amin
   New Mind Productions 1981

9. Freemasonry Ancient Egypt and the Islamic Destiny
   Mustafa El-Amin
   New Mind Productions 1988

10. <u>Abraham's Legacy,</u> Mustafa El-Amin
    New Mind Productions 1988

11. <u>African American Freemasons</u>: Why They Should
    Accept Al-Islam
    New Mind Productions 1990